CARL A. RUDISILL LIBRARY
LENOIR-RHYNE COLLEGE

From Sea Cliff to Barcelona

sketches and text by

Frank O. Braynard, F.R.S.

Dedicated to Barbara Baird

ISBN: 1-879-180-11

INTRODUCTION

EVER since 1923, when I made a sketch of the *Leviathan,* I have loved to draw. This new book is a collection of 200 sketches made in many places, sketches that have sat unused in my portfolios. Many years ago Robert B. Baird generously sponsored *A Tugman's Sketchbook.* He used it as a tool to let his customers know about his company. A year later, Bob telephoned to say he was pleased with the good will the book had brought, adding that he would like to help out with another. The result was *From Fire Island to Venice.* I never forgot this help, and a couple of years ago I wrote to him saying that I had a new book of sketches and would he be my patron once again. To my joy a cheerful "yes" followed. I am certainly fortunate in having such a friend as Robert Baird. It is with much gratitude that I dedicate this new work to his wife Barbara.

Travel has been one of my wife Doris' and my favorite joys. We have been fortunate in that both of us have had "something" to offer the cruise lines, meaning that we have been invited to sail on many cruises as guests. Doris brings her videos of great operas and offers them with introductions about the singers and the productions. I give talks on great liners and tall ships, offering videos of *Operation Sail 1976* and about famous ocean passenger vessels. We have made many wonderful cruises and these sketches are a result. There is one major area that is not covered in this work because it is on my list as a separate book, one which I hope will be published before too long. This will be entitled *Sketches in England and Ireland.*

Here are the places where my sketches were made.

Sketches done outside the United States

Anguilla 7
Antigua 7
Argentina 8–13
Austria 14–22
Brazil 23–26
British Virgin Islands 27–31
Canada 32–33
Chile 34–35
Estonia 36
France 37–43
Germany 44–49
Gibraltar 50
Greek Islands 51–54
Italy 55–58
Japan 59–61
Malta 62–63
Martinique 64
Mexico 65–66
Morocco 67
Norway 68–82
Nova Scotia 83
Patris to Brindisi 84–85
Peru 86–89
Poland 90–91
Portugal 92–99
Russia 100–110
Spain 111–117
St. Thomas 118
Turkey 121
Vancouver–Alaska 122–129

Sketches done in the United States

Bar Harbor 130
Fire Island 131–141
Glen Cove 142–143
Kings Point 144–147
New Orleans 148
Riverside 149
Sea Cliff 150–159
U.S. Virgin Islands 160–164

Sketches of Ocean and Sky 165–171

Other books by Frank Braynard 173

Looking out toward the Atlantic from our suite at the Carimar Beach Club, Anguilla, this is what we saw. Anguilla is a happy island of about 9,000 inhabitants. It has strong ties with Great Britain, including driving cars on the left. My second sketch was done while at Antigua, much more densely populated than Anguilla. I made this drawing while my wife Doris had a lovely swim.

Next comes the first two of several quick sketches of a trip through the Strait of Magellan made aboard the *Santa Magdalena* in 1983. It was a quick impression made as we entered the Patagonian Channels. The Strait is shown as a wide body of water. When my wife and I completed this cruise at Callao, Peru, the ship's master, Capt. Kenneth J. Sommers, dumbfounded me by giving me the charts he had used going through the Strait. They have been helpful in writing these captions.

Next was a narrow passage near Collingwood Strait and below Isla Carrington. To our south was the Isla Newton. What stories these great names hold. What a fascinating scene—one of the most thrilling in all the world. On both sides hills piled on top of hills and mountains atop mountains. A blanket of white-gray clouds appeared, slowly lowering until they obscured the tops of the tallest peaks.

The Strait became much more narrow. Between Escala Alta and the Guia Narrows the charts show a width descending from 600 feet to 73 feet. This drawing was done at Pto. Ochovairo, between Hanover Island and Isla Chatham. We were two-thirds of the way through and the weather remained good.

Going through the dangerous Shoal Passage, just below the Gray Channel, we came upon a gruesome sight. At first it appeared to be a tilted mass of metal, the stern of a ship three-quarters under water. As we got closer, a smokestack could be seen and a propeller. A portion of her keel was out of water and showing. Two-thirds of the vessel was underwater. She had Grace Line colors on her single stack (a black band at the top, with a thin white band and the rest green). We learned that she was the *Santa Leonora.*

By now we were two-thirds of the way through the day-long transit. The Strait widened out considerably. Rocks were everywhere, telling how dangerous things could be in fog or storm. Despite the layer of clouds, our weather could not have been nicer. We passed through Innocents Channel and Isla Farrel and were heading for Isla Robert. There must have been a thousand big and little islands in the Strait. The sea was calm.

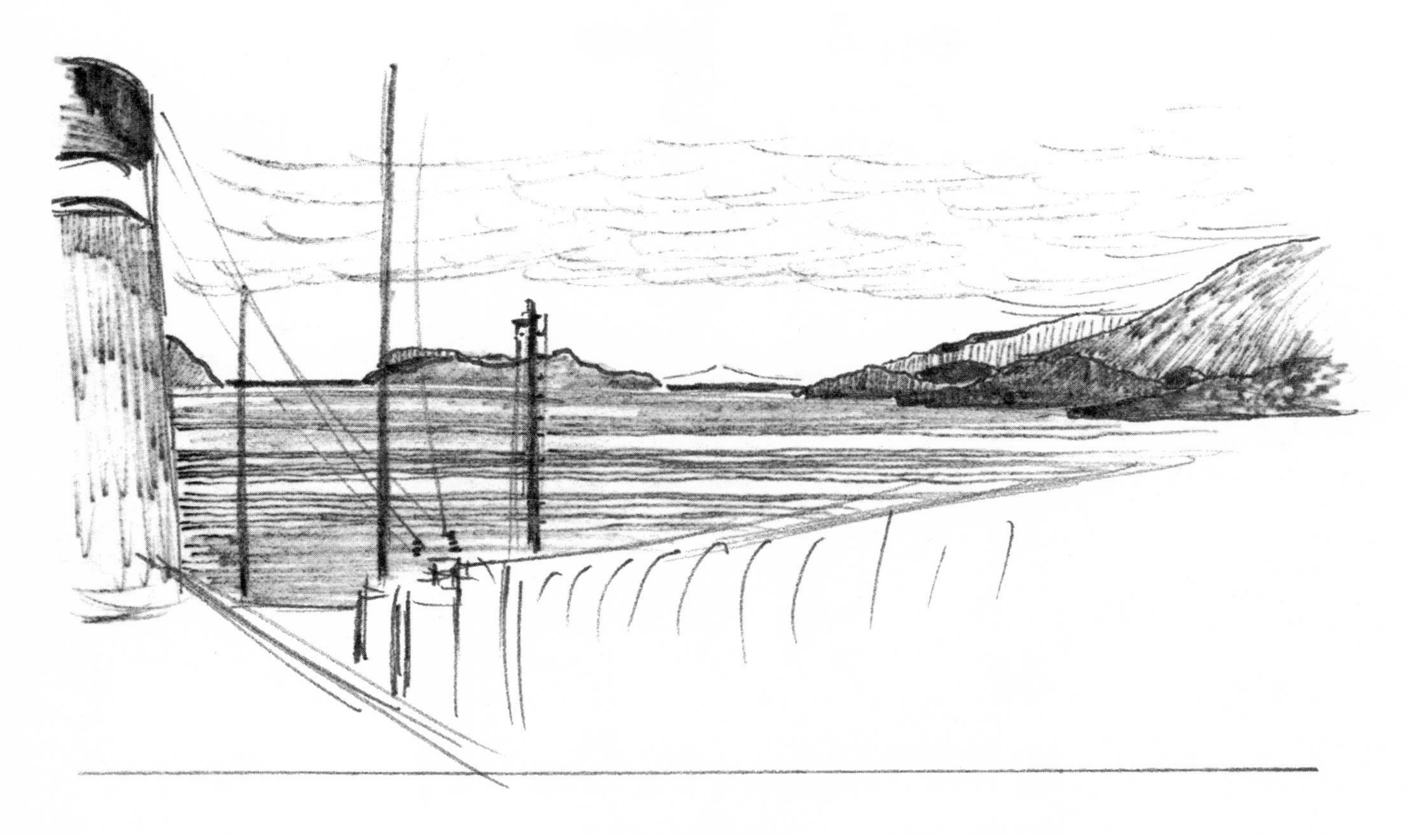

As we steamed through Conception Channel, I went up to the top deck forward of our ship's single smokestack and looked back. In my sketch I used the funnel as the the left margin and the rising superstructure as my lower right subject matter. Then we went throught Innocents Channel, as the Strait widened and we headed out toward the Pacific Ocean.

Sketching opportunities were everywhere in Austria. This was a delicious scene in Grinsing, where we had lunch one day. The onion dome struck me as especially beautiful. My flomaster pen was working well.

Another distinctive onion dome was part of the Gnigel Kirk, at Obergnigel, near Salzburg.

Salzburg's St. Sebastian Church graveyard is where Mozart's mother is buried.

Our hotel restaurant in Salzburg had a setting right out of a fairy tale.

I wanted to use the Bishops' Castle in Salzburg as a background for a sketch of the tower of St. Peter's Church, but I needed a vantage point above street level. Some kind people at the Ropertina Gallery permitted me to use their second story window, not knowing me from Adam.

The Bishops' Castle and a part of old Salzburg from across the river that divides the city into two parts.

Hearing the Vienna Boys' Choir at their own rehearsal hall.

We heard them a second time, seated in a box in the chapel of the Hofburg Palace.

Three views inside St. Stephen's Cathedral, Vienna, follow.

The third of these was made looking toward the organ pipes. I began it when I had difficulty seeing because there was so little light. Suddenly the sun came out and a wonderful reflection appeared on the stone wall just ahead of me, giving life to the scene.

Four drawings done in Rio de Janeiro come next. First the famous Sugar Loaf, all by itself. It was striking. I made this sketch from the lawn of the Museum of Modern Art. We took a bus to the top of Corcovada to see the great cross there.

I did three very quick sketches on the way up. The first was an unusually jagged mountain top, with the Atlantic behind it. Then we changed from our taxi to a bus and I had time for a quick panorama. Note the skyscrapers in the distance below the sea. They are tall buildings, but, I must admit, they look like little fence posts here.

Finally a vista of great peaks seen from below the cross (which I did not sketch), looking out over the fenced parking lot atop Corcovada.

In Santos harbor we passed a sunken freighter. Her name was *Vento.* The drawing was made from the starboard promenade deck of the passenger-cargo ship *Americana.*

Seven drawings made on the British Virgin Islands come next. First, a beach scene done on Great St. James. Then a close-up of rocks and a sailing craft drawn on Norman Island, said to be the setting for the famous book "Treasure Island." Hawk's Nest Beach follows on St. John's Island. To sketch this I sat under some bushes and somehow was bitten by a bug. I had red spots all over for a week. Next, a visit to Anagada, where we met a grand old man who was building his own boat. I thought he would make a good story but I could never sell it to anyone.

FRANK BRAYNARD
'89

FRANK O. BRAYNARD
'89

We moved over to Virgin Gorda and I had tremendous fun doing this scene of huge boulders on the beach. The area was part of Spanish Town and was called "the baths."

The small island of Prickly Pear is part of Virgin Gorda. We were aboard the *Caribbean Prince*, one of the few American-flag cruise ships in service, seen here at anchor. A view from her after deck shows another beach on Prickly Pear Island.

Another lovely cruise took Doris and me to Quebec. The old French quarter has been beautifully restored. It leads down to the water. These two drawings were fun because of the profusion of dormer windows and chimneys.

FRANK O. BRAYNARD
'86

This is Valparaiso, Chile, looking down from the rim of the hill around the port. Look closely between the building on the left and the telephone pole and you can see a bus roof and cars on the street far below. In our next sketch the upper end of an outdoor elevator that goes sideways as it goes up can be seen. Such elevators bring people from the seaport level to the main part of the city. It was so shaky and badly maintained that upon boarding it I wished that I had not. But we made it. It was common to see extra stories added atop regular buildings to accommodate more people. Look at the third of these three drawings and you can see what I mean. Atop the hill I found a long line of people waiting in front of a huge building. It turned out that the place was a jail and the people were visiting relatives who were inmates.

FRANK
BRAYNARD

Old Tallinn was right out of the Middle Ages. We found, however, that Estonia was very modern in its outlook, far ahead of the Soviet Union. We were there in 1973 trying to start an Operation Sail event in connection with the upcoming Olympics. The idea seemed to be going places when President Carter prohibited the U.S. from participating in the Olympics.

On a recent visit to Albert Brenet, noted French artist and friend, we had a hotel in an old part of Paris. I did these two sketches from our hotel window. The first sketch shows at the left a modern skyscraper which destroys the feeling of old dormers and tin-roofed buildings—but you cannot get in the way of progress, I guess. Several marvelous chimneys, jam-packed with chimney pots, add to the flavor of the other drawing. Brenet's home was at 41 Rue Le Courbe. When I worked for Moran Towing, he did many superb egg tempera paintings of new ships that came into New York harbor, docked, of course, by Moran tugs with the famous "White M" on their smokestacks. I had ten wonderful years with that company, going on tugs almost daily. What a job that was.

We stayed at the Hotel Provencal in Villefranche, overlooking the harbor. Villefranche has all the charm and none of the tourist problems that nearby Nice has. We were there a week and have been dying to go back ever since. We often ate meals on the roof where the beach umbrellas are. There was a lovely outdoor dining room around the palm tree at a lower level, and an indoor dining room just inside the hotel facing out onto where the palm tree stood.

A few steps down a gentle hill and this is what you saw. The bells from this church's bell tower rang every fifteen minutes. The red tile roofs and green shutters of the neighborhood made it a colorful scene. We often had hot chocolate in the little restaurant behind this wonderful old tree. I loved that town.

The backs of houses on Ave. Sadi Carnot looked out over this gully. A small open area called Square Jardin Francois Binon fronted on another side. We often ate at a small restaurant on this square. The weather was perfect, the pen was under control, and everything seemed to work together while we were in Villefranche. The sketches I made there are among my all-time favorites.

This drawing includes buildings dating back six hundred years. Note the Moorish influence evident in the pointed arch at the far end of this street, which was called Rue de May. The street is a series of wide terraces.

This massive moat has not seen water for many years. But the ancient portcullis is still very real, and, I believe, can be made to operate. The next picture is of the street scene at Eze, a small town we visited while at Villefranche.

A superb old tree and a lovely square not far from our hotel. We often got hot chocolate at the little restaurant behind the tree.

One other sketch made in the Villefranche area is included here. It is of Cap Ferrat, overlooking the mountains of Beaulieu and Eze. Even the appealing light pole seems to fit in. The French make most artistic light poles.

One of the most fascinating assignments I ever had was doing a book about the new cruise liner *Crown Odyssey.* She was being constructed in Germany at a small town named Papenburg, close to the Dutch border. The main street was a canal. I drew it. It was nice to see a row of new trees planted at the right of the canal. It was hard to imagine that only a mile away there were 1,500 highly skilled men working on the rising hull of the 50,000-ton liner. I had some spare time and sketched a close-up of one of the typical leeboard barges approaching a footbridge, one that could be raised to permit her to pass through.

The new ship was being built by the Meyer Werft (yard) within the world's largest covered ways. My first drawing, made from a balcony above the floor of the ways, showed the new ship's stern. A second drawing showed the bow, minus the great stem, which lay upside down nearby. A third drawing zoomed in on the bulbous bow. It would be hoisted into place as a single unit. We got to know three generations of the Meyer family, owners of the shipyard. Pericles S. Panagopoulos, owner of Royal Cruise Line, for which the ship was being built, was there. We had many good chats with him. We also spent much time with his son and daughter, who were there and keenly interested in the new ship.

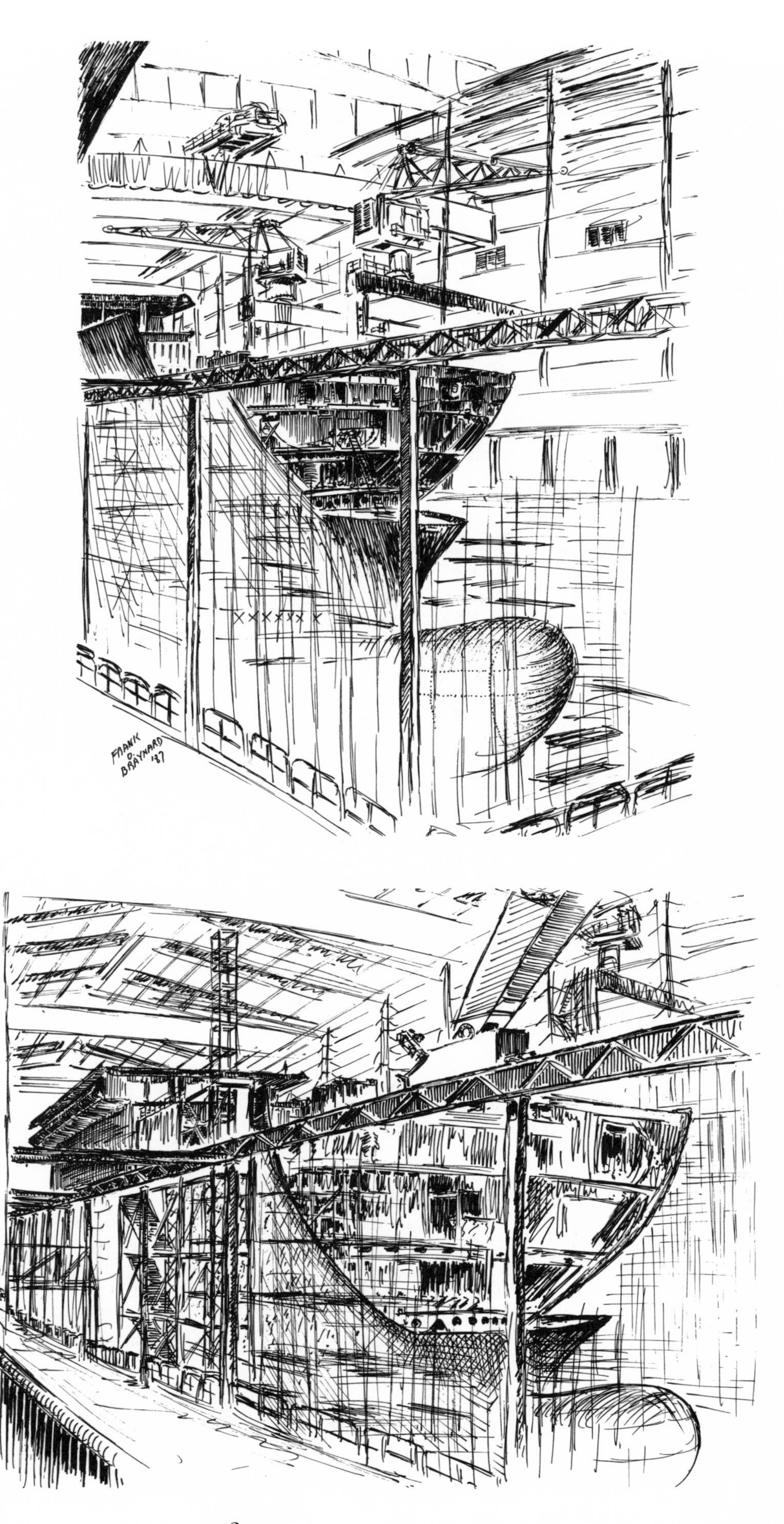
FRANK O. BRAYNARD '87

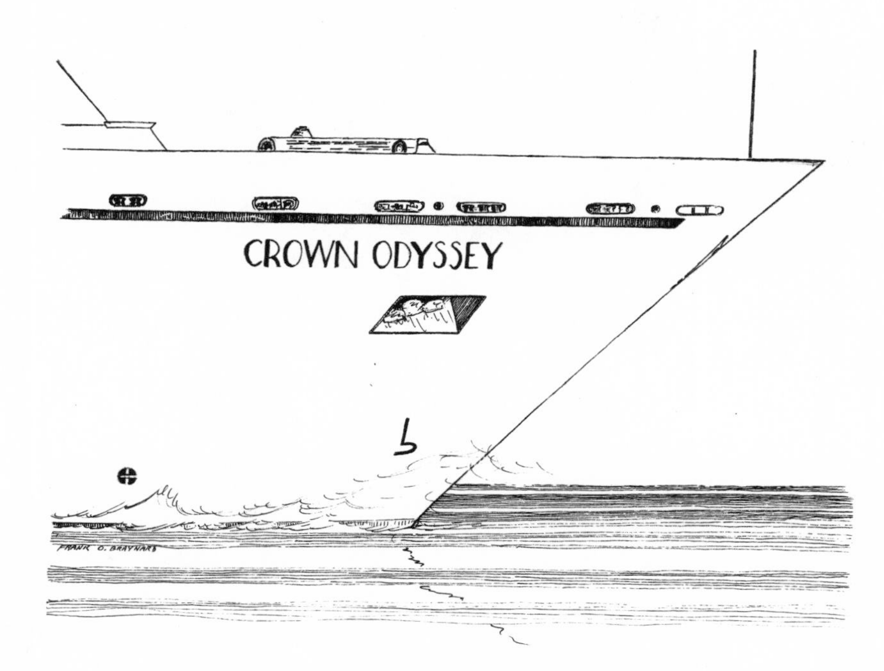

I made several sketches from conversations with shipyard people and a study of the ship's blueprints. One was of the stern as it would look when finished, with large windows in the hull in place of portholes. Royal Cruise was a pioneer in this revolutionary concept. I drew the sleek clipper bow, a design which went back to the *Normandie.* And I had fun sketching the "Top of the Crown" lounge forward of the smokestack and high above the bridge. A 360-degree view could be had from this area, which included two rooms. Their windows slanted out (from bottom to top) at such an angle that there had to be a railing to keep you from falling into them. Then I drew a side elevation, showing the starboard of the ship as she would look when finished. Finally I made a "fish eye" conception of what she would be like at sea, a somewhat exaggerated view along the lines of artists Fred Hoertz and Worden Wood.

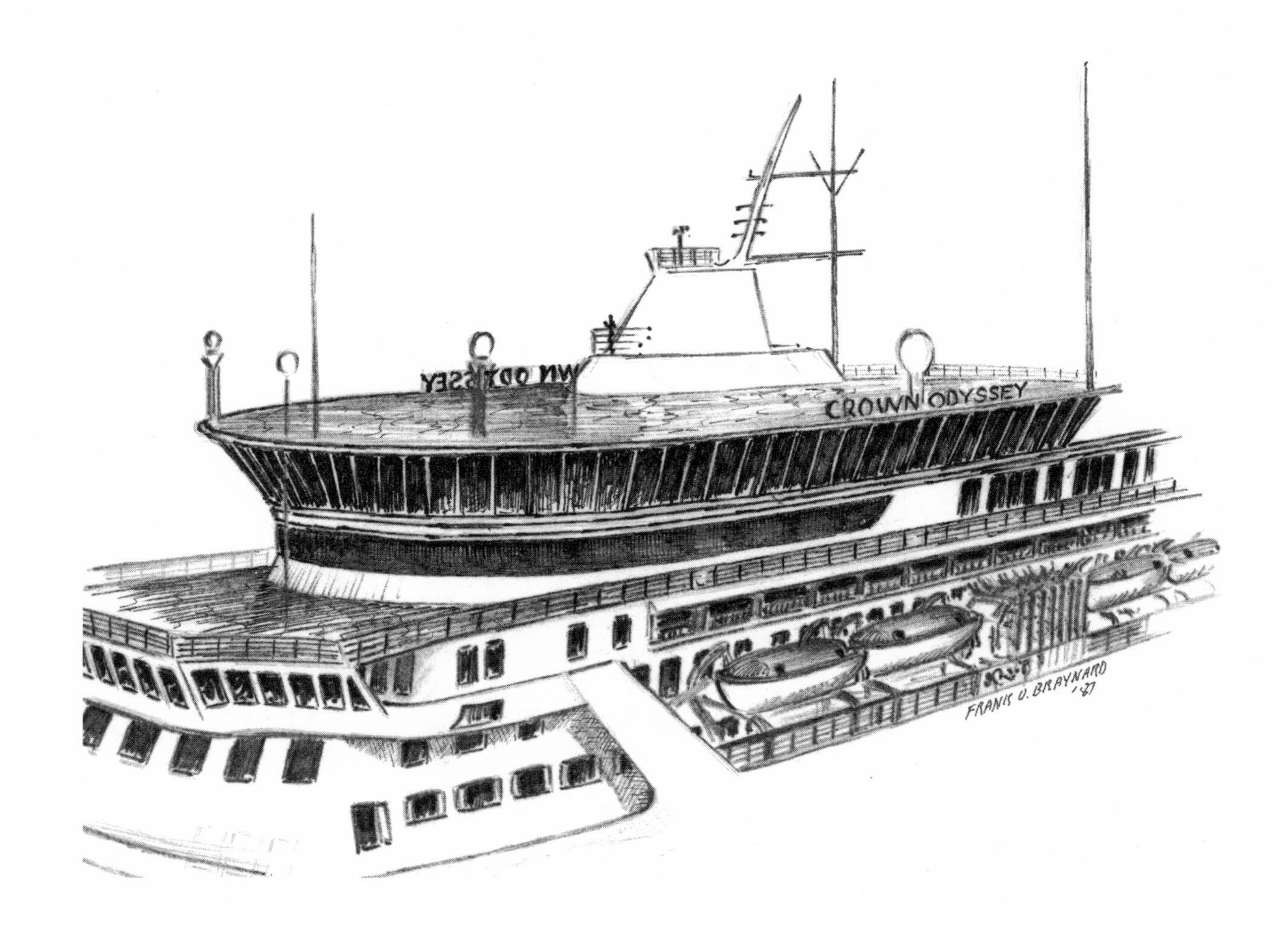
CROWN ODYSSEY
FRANK O. BRAYNARD '87

CROWN ODYSSEY
FRANK O. BRAYNARD '87

CROWN ODYSSEY
CROWN ODYSSEY
FRANK BRAINARD

Moving on to another trip, this drawing shows how we tied up next to several oil tanks when we docked at Gibraltar. I must say I thought twice before including the sketch. It shows the rock of Gibraltar from a different angle.

We had a sumptuous cruise to some of the Greek Islands aboard the beautiful four-masted square rigger *Sea Cloud.* One picture done on each of five islands is offered here. Let's take them alphabetically. At Delos we missed the first tender and I used the time waiting for the next one making this sketch. Next is a street corner on Hydra, a few blocks in from the water. I enjoyed doing that telephone pole. Wood is always fun to sketch. Making the shadows was fun.

While doing this next drawing on Mykonos, I started chatting with an American from some other ship who stopped when he saw me sketching. He stunned me by suddenly saying: "Is Ed Braynard your brother?" Yes, I replied. It is a small world. We would have gone up to the top of Santorini by donkey, but chose the cable car. The whole beautiful city is built along one street on the top of a ridge. Again, it was hard to pick what to sketch.

This waterfront at Symi was fun to do.

But most rewarding was getting back on the ship and copying a grand photo of her under full canvas. What a beauty she is.

I am including only 5 sketches made in Italy. Others of my books have more, but these have never been published before. Two of these are views of Puerto Ercole, Sardinia. The first shows the fort high on a hill and the little town below to the right. Getting nearer I did a close-up of the fort and part of the town.

Tourists usually rush through Civitavecchia en route to Rome. We thought it would be fun to linger. The next drawing is one of fishing boats tied up in the harbor there. The six-sided fort at the top left was designed by Michelangelo.

We enjoyed lunch in an out-of-the-way eating place in Venice and this scene grabbed me. The restaurant's name may have been "Ottoprova." See the letters that show through on their awning.

Looking over a narrow canal, we see a hotel entrance. This was not our hotel. We stayed at the Saturnia, nearby.

The wonderful castle at Osaka was a challenge. So strange, so big, so very demanding. My first sketch shows a full view. I walked around it and found another smaller structure, with a lovely tree embracing it and a grand shadow on the stone wall inside the moat. My third Osaka drawing was of Naknoshima Island. I did it from the Naniwa-Su Ji Ave. Bridge. The barges in the foreground make the sketch, I think.

FRANK O. BRAYNARD

Frank Braynard
11,28,82

Malta is another sketcher's paradise. I have four drawings to show. The first was a stairway to nowhere. I walked to the top and could go no farther. The wall was a barrier. A suggestion of an arch incorporated into the wall was evidence that there had been an entrance at one time. I drew the harbor from the pier where our ship tied up, then crossed it in a ferry and drew it from the other side. The city's name was Valletta. My fourth drawing was a sketch that looked into the inner recesses of the port.

FRANK BRAYNARD '85
MALTA
VALLETTA Harbor

A magnificent setting for a beautiful structure. Someone's dream come true. This was a one-third size replica of the famous Sacre Coeur Cathedral of Paris. It is in Balata, Martinique. When entering I was surprised to find that it had no floor, just dirt.

We escaped from a busy Puerta Vallarta, Mexico, to do this sketch at a nearby beach.

Acapulco is another very popular spot for tourists. This old tree outside the Fort San Diego's moat drew our attention. The moat has been well preserved, as this third Acapulco drawing shows.

While I was drawing this at Tangier, Morocco, Doris disappeared into the Casbah. Fortunately, she found her own way out. The times were out of joint right then, as it was only a few days after the attack on the *Achille Lauro*, when a crippled American passenger in a wheelchair was thrown overboard by terrorists. When we landed at Tangier the port was crowded with men with machine guns. Divers went under our hull to look for explosives at each port we came to. I drew my own shadow and that of a palm tree I was standing under, which can be seen at the bottom of the drawing.

We have taken the coastal express steamer voyage up and back from Bergen to around the North Cape three times over the years. I will show drawings done in 10 Norwegian places: Bergen, Torvik, Molde, Ornes, Bode, Svolvaer, Tromso, Hammerfest, the North Cape and Kirkenes. A few of my sketches, sad to say, have no locations written on the back. I scold myself for being so careless. Let's start with the first two ports. One is of a small ship being built at Bergen. I wish I had had time to find out more about her. Two scenes in Torvik are here. One, a port view with one of those ultra seaworthy Norse double enders at a pier. The other is a winter view done in 1988 as we steamed by in our coastal express motorship, the *Vesteralen.* Such wonderful memories.

FRANK O. BRAYNARD
'88

I have four sketches from our steamer next. The first is out of a forward window while docked at Molde. It was March and everyone thought we were crazy to take the trip at that time. The weather was perfect except for one day of snow at Vardo, northeast of the North Cape. My next sketch is from Ornes, a port well above the tree-line. You can see nothing but polished rock. A dream world. Then two views of Bode, one showing our ship approaching, and the other the actual port, with some surprisingly modern buildings. I like the transparent mist cloud cover.

F. BRAYNARD - '88

FRANK BRAYNARD

Fishing boat at her pier.

A reporter on a local newspaper was doing a book on spies and code breaking. Bob and Rhoda Amon, two old friends who went with us on our 1988 costal trip, knew this chap. He needed a drawing for a new book. The book would describe how off the Skraaven Lighthouse on Flesa Island, near Svolvaer, the British had captured a receiving set for the Enigma code machine. It was locked in the master's desk of a sinking German craft, and found at the very last possible moment by a British naval officer. I do not know whether the reporter ever used the sketch, but I have used his story many times in lectures.

Then another of my sketches done aboard the *Vesteralen* in 1987. This one was made looking back over the stern. Doris and I used this drawing for our Christmas card that year.

Next let's show two sketches, one from Tromso and the other from Hammerfest, both north of the Arctic Circle. The "Cathedral of the North" at Tromso was a must for us. I was amazed at its superb stained glass window at the altar end of the church and made a very, very quick impression in pen and ink. Leaving Hammerfest I drew the much more finished picture of the *Vesteralen*'s bow. It was such fun to do and turned out so nicely that it seems like only yesterday that we were there.

The North Cape comes next. My sketch is partly from imagination, we were moving so rapidly in the cold, cold water. I remembered vividly being on top of it on our first trip and starting to throw a small stone off and down into the water. I suddenly had the feeling that I might follow the stone off the top simply from momentum so I kept turning and threw the stone in the other direction.

Known as “the horn” this rocky formation is just around the North Cape.

The Nidaros Cathedral, Trondheim, a magnificent structure begun in the 11th Century. It fell into disrepair, only to be restored over the past century. Funds for its construction are said to have been sent home by William the Conqueror. This drawing was originally made for my book *Search for the Tall Ships*, published in 1977.

The passion to sketch overcame me on one trip and I could not resist copying a very fine photograph that I found in a travel booklet. It showed a typical Norse fishing boat entering a fjord in rough weather.

Our final stop on all these trips was at Kirkenes. I did this drawing in March 1988, standing on the rooftop of Europe. Naturally, I could not use gloves, but the cold did not seem to bother me. The drawing took about two hours, maybe a little less.

A cruise to Montreal included a stop at Halifax, on Nova Scotia. We did not have long, but I went ashore and sketched this attractive old home. I remember I had to rush back to the ship because I spent so much time on the drawing.

We took a great cruise that ended in Athens one time. Determined not to fly any more than possible, we got back to London over sea and land. By bus we traveled to Patris, on the west coast of Greece. There we boarded the elegant Italian ferry *Egnatia,* a really fine vessel, and sailed via Corfu to Brindisi, near the foot of Italy. I made these three drawings and then we went by train up the entire length of Italy and across France. We took a hovercraft across the Channel—awful—and then a train to London. I don't think I ever enjoyed a steamer trip more than our ride on this lovely *Egnatia.*

It took me so long to make this sketch of the ruins at Machu Piccu that I hardly had any time to see this wonderful, scary place. We were on top of a tall peak in the Andes Mountains, with thousands of feet straight down on all sides. But it was worth it. The Spaniards never found the Incas who took refuge up here. The place was called the "lost city" for centuries, only being discovered relatively recently. It is in Peru. The following three drawings were made while we descended from Machu Piccu. They give three views of the Urubamba River which starts high in the Andes and then runs into the Amazon.

FRANK
BRAYNARD

Polish castles and churches have always fascinated me. In preparation for a visit to Poland during Operation Sail days I made a few sketches of Polish buildings. Both are churches, but what churches—so different from churches in other lands. One is at Gniew and the other is in Wigry. It is my ambition to visit both these fascinating buildings and make more sketches.

We sailed twice across the Atlantic on the little liner *Polaris*. These two drawings were made on our 1993 crossing. Of just over 2,000 gross tons, the *Polaris* can accommodate only 80 passengers. She is a beauty and a very good sea boat, as they say. Here I am standing forward. My sketch is of the ship's bell and foredeck. The next view is from the Lounge, aft on the Upper Deck. I am looking at our lifeboat out of the large portside window. We only had 35 passengers aboard on our voyage from Antigua to Lisbon.

NASSAU
MB=3.00M
FRANK O. BRAYNARD '93

These six drawings were made at Funchal, Madeira. Funchal harbor is strikingly beautiful. The fishing boat is landing, as a sailor at the bow tests the depth with an oar. Along the walk into town we passed this lovely spot. Funchal Cathedral has brown stone up and down its corners. Note the elegant tile pavement in the square in the foreground. Cobblestone streets add charm. Two quick sketches of the land as we leave.

Phoebus
FRANK BRAYNARD '85

BB
BLANDY BROTHERS & CO. LTD.
FRANK BRAYNARD '85

FRANK BRAYNARD
85

This is the massive "Old Cathedral" of Lisbon. Up on a hill to the right of the main center of town, the building was badly damaged in an earthquake several hundred years ago, and has never been fully repaired. Note the corrugated iron roofing of the two massive supporting piles on either side of the transepts around the stained glass window. Despite its condition, this is one of the most awe-inspiring cathedrals I have ever seen. Note also the almost moorish battlements atop the highest portions near the front. Another Lisbon cathedral was almost completely demolished by the same earthquake. We are so fortunate that this survived.

A view from our hotel window in Odessa in 1977. We were beginning the first of two grand tips on the Don-Volga rivers. The Odessa Cathedral is shown in the center, with the Opera House hinted at off in back to the left, only its roof and spire showing. We led a group of 165 people on this riverboat cruise. The Russians could not have been more friendly. Going through the Don-Volga Canal was most interesting. High cliffs and hills were on our left as we went up toward Kazan.

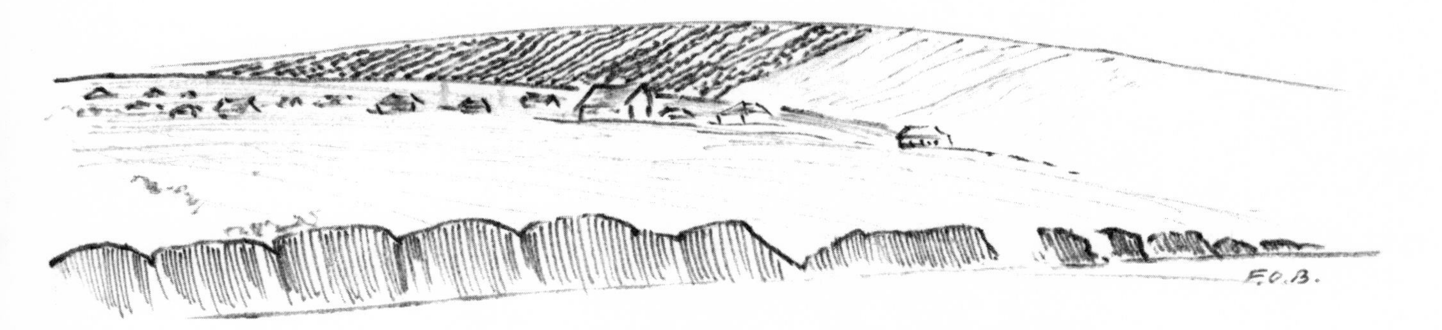

Cliffs, sometimes really high ones, were on our left as we went up the Volga. We were aboard the *Maxim Gorky*, a really palatial new riverboat. She was built in Austria, but "to Russian plans," we were told. The land to the right as we went up river was flat. Most of the time we saw nothing but fields and trees. We often stopped and went ashore. On one such landing I climbed up the bank and sketched the river and flat shore on the other side.

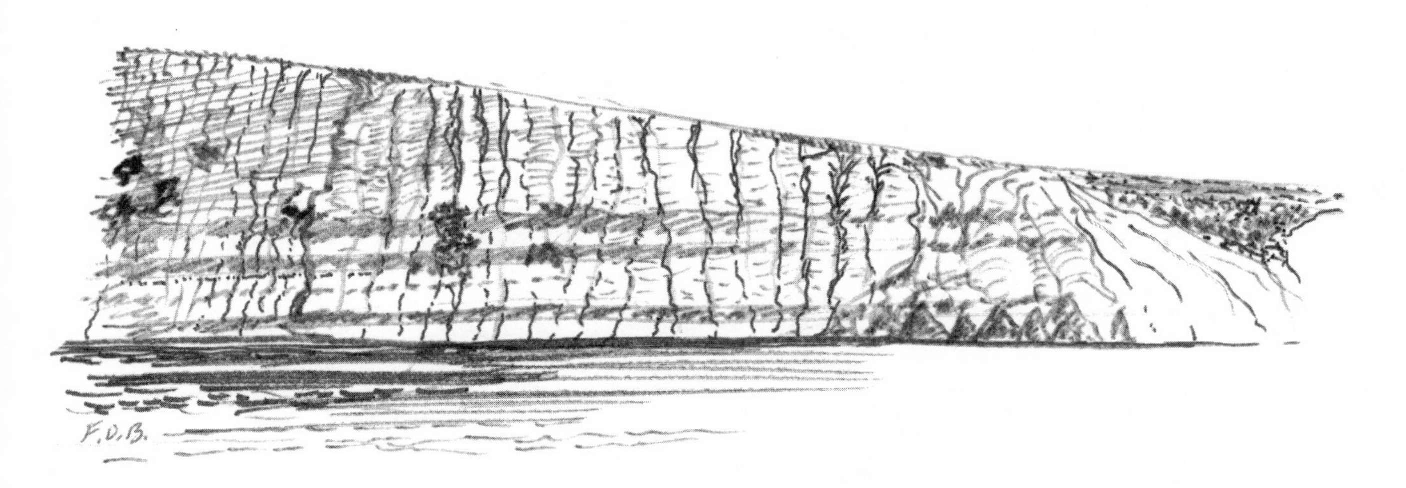

Here I sketched one of the small towns we passed on the Volga. The people everywhere were friendly, smiling and eager to visit with us. We tied up at Zhiguli for fuel, and I made two sketches, being bothered a lot by swarms of mosquitoes.

The river trip ended at Kazan. I sketched that ancient city's cathedral. We enjoyed our stay there and learned a lot.

Two drawings done in St. Petersburg, known then as Leningrad, are used here. One is the Cathedral of Peter and Paul, whose spire I was amazed at because it was so tall and thin. The other was the famous Russian cruiser *Aurora,* whose crew helped start the Revolution. I found to my delight that the library had a copy of my book on the pioneer steamship *Savannah,* which had sailed to St. Petersburg in 1819.

For some reason I was overwhelmed by the Cathedral at Majorca (Mallorca), and could not bring myself to try a front view. It is a grand structure, let me say.

The Canary Islands could, of course, provide sketches for an entire book. I have five here: two from Tenerife, two from Lanzarote and one from Las Palmas. These islands are very close to Africa. I will never forget a demonstration that a guide gave us. It was on Lanzarote. He scraped the earth we were walking on and then asked Doris to drop a tissue. It burst into flame so hot was the ground. The first sketch in this group shows the mountains and modern buildings. I drew it from the stern deck of our ship. The next drawing is a typical street scene with an old tree with roots clutching out in a wide circle. Next is what was called the Castilo de S. Gabriel at Arrecife. Everything is made of cinder blocks from lava eruptions. I should have stopped sooner with this sketch. The temptation is always to do just another brick or two. More cinder block here, in this tiny harbor with its pull-up entrance for small boats with masts. The fifth drawing is of three rusty bows tied up together at a pier. I was standing alone on the pier and as I drew, several tough-looking characters clustered around me. I was alarmed. But they turned out to be eager to see the sketch and were very cordial.

FARMACIA
ANALISIS
FRANK BRAYNARD '85

FRANK
BRAYNARD
'85

FRANK
BRAYNARD
'85

Now the drawing that inspired this book, and after which the book is named. The Temple Expiatori De La Sagrada Familia, of Barcelona. It was begun in 1882 and will take another century to complete. If you consider the great model of the finished structure, the portion completed today is about 30%, but it still is one of the grandest, most thrilling pieces of architecture on this globe. I only pray it can someday be completed. Doris and I went up in an elevator to a height of about 200 feet, using a tower behind this facade that can barely be seen in this sketch. The Cathedral was designed by Antonio Gaudi, whose full name was Antonio Gaudi Cornet. He was given charge in 1883 and gave his whole life to the effort. I must go back to see more.

We were aboard the QE2 on a cruise when this drawing was made. It is a scene at St. Thomas, with the Cunarder out in the bay. Her stack looks taller than it really is because of foreshortening.

The amphitheater at Ephesus can still be used. St. Paul was there and many early Christians, not to mention Anthony and Cleopatra. It was a place of wonder. The massive castle at Bodrum is another treasure from the past. Much of it is intact. Sketch 148 shows a close-up within the walls.

FRANK O. BRAYNARD
'90

FRANK O. BRAYNARD

The "Sky Ride" at Prince Rupert was a thrill. After Victoria the shore seemed to look rougher and more rugged. The water seemed smoother.

Approaching Margerie Glacier in Tarr Inlet. There was ice in the water and the hills were becoming mountains. Margerie Glacier was dropping into the water at what seemed an amazing rate. The ice was blue. The third sketch shows the west side of Tarr Inlet.

No vegetation of any visible kind as our ship reaches the Muir Glacier. Small islands covered with pine trees spotted the passage. The Mendenhall Glacier was, if possible, more dramatic than any of the others.

Bow on view of the *Regent Star*, ex *Statendam*.

My felt tip Flomaster pen was doing itself proud when I left the old *Royal Odyssey* at Bar Harbor, Maine. The tide was low, and you can see how far down from this sketch. Can you find the *Royal Odyssey*?

Our cottage at 100 Surf Walk is only this far from Great South Bay. Go the other way and you reach the Atlantic Ocean in perhaps 10 minutes. Our village is called Saltaire, one of a number of attractive communities on this 40-mile strip of sand. Looking toward the ocean from the porch and you see this view, several small lots separating us from the closest house. Many houses are 75 or so years old. Here is a modern one. We believe ours was built around 1911. It is stained red and we love it. For some reason I have never made a really good sketch of it. This is our "fisherman's pier" and I drew it because shadows on wood are made for my kind of pen.

FRANK
BRAYNARD

FRANK BRAYNARD

An ocean front house like this attractive one at Saltaire is risky because of the danger of damage to the dunes in very bad storms such as were had in 1992 and 1993. The older house here has had quite a history. It was raised up and floated from the ocean front all the way down to the Bay in the 1939 storm. Then it was brought back and again put on the dunes. Later it was turned around to face the walk. Still later it was moved a little inland and away from the dunes. But in our most recent storms the dunes were destroyed, the house was undermined and fell onto the beach where it was, sad to say, broken into kindling wood by the waves.

I love the tree leaning over this grand old home. Mike Coffee, architect and builder, was responsible for many of the older homes in Saltaire. We are proud to have a Coffee house. The one shown here is also a Coffee house.

Modern architecture is also represented in Saltaire. This home has weathered well.

Here are two views of the Church of Our Lady of the Sea in Saltaire. It is a Catholic Church. Next, a drawing of the Saltaire Episcopal Church.

FRANK
BRAYNARD

F.Q.B.

A final drawing for the Fire Island section is my sketch of the walk to the lighthouse. It takes about 40 minutes to get there. On days when the lighthouse is open, climbing to the top is a most exciting thing to do. Special permission is required.

A drawing I made in 1939 showing our family home in Glen Cove, where I lived from 1922 until 1949. Although I was born in Sea Cliff, my physician father decided that he might find more work in Glen Cove and we moved there. Look through the brick entrance and you can see the lovely Georgian-style house he built. The other drawing done in my Glen Cove days is a sketch of the Hempstead Harbour Club. The Club has always used the English way of spelling "harbor." I believe I did this drawing in 1939.

The first two drawings show the schooner *Mazurka,* which was given to the U.S. Merchant Marine Academy at Kings Point, L.I., N.Y. and then sold. The first sketch shows the Throgs Neck Bridge in the right background. I have been curator of the American Merchant Marine Museum at the Academy since 1979. The next drawing shows a row of sloops that the men and women midshipmen train with. Sketch 175 shows the Academy Chapel overlooking Great Neck Bay as well as the *Mazurka.* The last of these Kings Point sketches is of the Walter P. Chrysler mansion, now the main administrative building of the Academy.

Sailing on the *Delta Queen* or the *Mississippi Queen* as often as Doris and I have, it has been our pleasure to get to know New Orleans. This sketch was made at breakfast one day. I looked out of the typical half-moon window and saw a typical New Orleans building with its own half-moon window and typical New Orleans shutters. And the lamppost with its old-style light also rang bells in my head. A sketch just had to follow—and did, just like two and two make four.

During my research for the *Leviathan* books, I discovered a gentleman who had served as a boy on this famous ship. His name was Albert Boyce and he invited Doris and me to his home in Riverside, Ca. This sketch resulted.

Sea Cliff is famous around the world for its beautifully preserved gingerbread houses. One of them is the Fischer House. Our first drawing shows the porch of this old home (at far right) and a view out over the bluff. Between the trees can be seen, if you look really hard, the Hempstead Harbour Yacht Club and its various wooden walks out to the boat float and the swimming float. A second view shows almost all of the Fischer House with its two towers. Again, the view out and over to the water is included. Glen Cove is on the hill rising in the distance. Two superb gingerbread houses come next, side by side on Glen Avenue. They are called the blue and the pink houses. Finally, the Hogarth home, with its two-story-high portcochere.

FRANK
BRAYNARD
'66

FRANK BRAYNARD '66

Arata's corner, named after a grocery store. The other side of the corner looks like a bank and was actually used as the setting for a bank in a film made in our village years ago. Two delightful "Gay Nineties" houses on Sea Cliff Avenue. When the third sketch here was done the first building was used as our Village Hall. I was a Village Trustee at that point and sat in state there on an old stage, as the place had also been the village motion picture theater. I never expected to find a way to use these drawings.

VILLAGE OF SEA CLIFF

Of traditional Russian architecture, St. Seraphim is on our "hill" overlooking Long Island Sound. The Church of Our Lady of Kazan is on the other side of the Village. Russians who originally used an old garage for their place of worship eventually restored it into the beautiful structure we know as Our Lady of Kazan. St. Seraphim was built from the ground up as a church. Russians from all over the area use both places. Icons and other hand-painted decorations fill these two churches.

The original yacht club had a pier at water level and a clubhouse atop the cliff, as shown here. It was on the side overlooking Port Washington. I made two drawings of the old Sea Cliff Yacht Club, but could find only one when this book started. Here it is. It shows how the club stretched out from our cliff into Hempstead Harbor. The actual clubhouse is on top of the hill beside the flagpole.

Five U.S. Virgin Islands drawings are next. First, Beef Island, with a sailboat; then the Tower of the Lutheran Church of St. Croix, as seen from across the street; next, inside the Fort Christiansted at St. Croix; next, schooner *Roseway*, of OpSail fame, bow onto the *Caribbean Prince*, our cruising vessel; and finally, the old bakery oven of the Sinbad Restaurant in the heart of St. Thomas.

FRANK O. BRAYNARD '84

FRANK O. BRAYNARD
89

FRANK O. BRAYNARD
'89

Seven different scenes, six original sketches, the last a printed copy of a sketch sold to Texaco.

Books by Frank O. Braynard

Lives of the Liners, 1947
Fifty Years of N.Y. Ship, 1949
Famous American Ships, 1956
The Story of Ships, 1962
S.S. Savannah, the Elegant Steamship, 1963
By Their Works Ye Shall Know Them, 1968
Leviathan, Vol. I, 1972
Marine Collection of India House, 1973
Leviathan, Vol. II, 1974
Leviathan, Vol. III, 1976
Leviathan, Vol. IV, 1978
Great Liners, 1978, with others
Famous American Ships, 1978, new edition
Sail, Steam & Splendor, 1978, with others
Romance of the Sea, 1980, with others
Leviathan, Vol. V, 1981
The Big Ship, 1981
Il Nastro Azzurro, 1981, in Italian
Fifty Famous Liners (first vol.), with Bill Miller, 1982
Leviathan, Vol. VI, 1983
Fifty Famous Liners, Vol. II, with Bill Miller, 1985
Picture History of the Normandie, 1987
Fifty Famous Liners, Vol. III, with Bill Miller, 1987
S.S. Savannah, new edition, 1988
Story of the Titanic in Postcards, 1988
Salute to the Crown, 1988
Classic Ocean Liners, Vol. I, 1990
Picture History of the Cunard Line, with Bill Miller, 1990
U.S. Steamships, 1991
Tall Ships of Today in Photographs, 1993
Classic Ocean Liners, Vol. II, 1994

Sketchbooks and Portfolios of Sketches

Ship Sketchbook, portfolio of 12 sketches, 1962
Tugman's Sketchbook, 1965
From Fire Island to Venice, 1966
One Square Mile—a Sea Cliff Sketchbook, 1967
1976 Operation Sail Portfolio
Search for the Tall Ships
American Troopships Past and Present
United States Passenger Ships Over the Years
A Sketcher's Paradise
Saltaire Sketches

Books in Preparation

Classic Ocean Liners, Vol. III, *Bremen & Europa* (Liberte)
U.K. Sketchbook
Ship Engravings of the 1860s From Harpers, Leslies, Illinois
London News Illustrated
Classic Ocean Liners, Vol. IV (*Manhattan* and *Washington*)